Heart Deep

THE JOURNEY of a LIGHT-WORKING EMCEE

SARAH CONNOR

BALBOA.
PRESS
A DIVISION OF HAY HOUSE

Balboa Press books may be ordered through booksellers or by contacting:

Balboa Press
A Division of Hay House
1663 Liberty Drive
Bloomington, IN 47403
www.balboapress.com
1-(877) 407-4847

ISBN: 978-1-4525-0555-8 (sc)
ISBN: 978-1-4525-0556-5 (e)

Because of the dynamic nature of the Internet, any web addresses or links contained in this book may have changed since publication and may no longer be valid. The views expressed in this work are solely those of the author and do not necessarily reflect the views of the publisher, and the publisher hereby disclaims any responsibility for them.

The author of this book does not dispense medical advice or prescribe the use of any technique as a form of treatment for physical, emotional, or medical problems without the advice of a physician, either directly or indirectly. The intent of the author is only to offer information of a general nature to help you in your quest for emotional and spiritual well-being. In the event you use any of the information in this book for yourself, which is your constitutional right, the author and the publisher assume no responsibility for your actions.

Any people depicted in stock imagery provided by Thinkstock are models, and such images are being used for illustrative purposes only.
Certain stock imagery © Thinkstock.

Printed in the United States of America

Balboa Press rev. date: 09/18/2012

Contents

Preface

When I first started writing poetry I never imagined that any would be published, most likely because I dreaded anyone reading my spelling mistakes and then getting so caught up with the misdemeanours, that they would fail to absorb the meaning of the poem. Yet, as time rolled on and more poetry flowed through me, I continued to scribble poetically into my journal and on scrap bits of paper (depending where I was when the poem arrived; at times I had to use toilet paper, just to get it down before it trundled away).

Ten years on, I have gathered enough poems for a book, and as I worked on accepting myself, I have gained more confidence with the idea of publishing. I thought 'there are hundreds and thousands of spelling police out there, I'll just ask some for help', and so I did. A huge thank you to Mia Churchett, Justine Benfell and Priya Singh for your patience and hours spent circling and correcting. I appreciate your kindness, friendship and support.

I would also like to thank David Lawson for his incredible talent and big heart in designing the cover of my book. An even bigger thank you to his big sister and my soul mate Jemma Lawson, who has worked alongside me for many gruelling hours of editing, correcting and most importantly supporting me in those moments of doubt. You really are the woman who wiped clean the butterfly's wings so it could fly once more.

To all those souls who have inspired me to write, some of you are no longer in my life but all of you will remain in my heart forever. Thank you for the journey we shared.

Last but not least, Tonia Kitchin. Thank you is not quite enough to express the gratitude I have felt for your presence in my life. Your gifts and insights have helped me find my inner child in the scary dark places I had left her years before. You held my hand as we entered those spaces and gave me the guidance and support needed to heal her little heart - bringing her home to love once more. Thank you for helping me believe in myself enough to allow my heart to shine again, giving it the confidence to sing its song to the world.

Heart Deep is a collection of poetry that was written over ten years - poetry about relationships, love, loss, family, friends, humanity and heartbreak.

I hope you enjoy reading this poetic journey as much as I have enjoyed being inspired to write it. No matter how painful at times the inspiration has come, in the end those experiences have been the most incredible and life-changing gifts; blessings that I would not change for the world, for they have helped me grow far beyond my imagination.

And for that, I am truly grateful.

Love and blessings to all.

Sarah Connor

Introduction

Being an easily distracted child, I struggled all the way through school. Behaviour suggestive of ADHD, coupled with mild dyslexia, I never believed I was good at anything to do with reading and writing, or school in general for that matter.

Let me take you back to the very beginning of my journey . . .

I have clear memories of my first writing assignment; I was 5 years old and sitting next to my friend in Grade One. I cannot remember her name, but she was very sweet, of Asian descent, focused and extremely diligent.

Our teacher had given us our first assignment - writing a poem. I had paid no attention whatsoever to the teacher's lengthy explanation, and it was only when she stopped instructing and said, "Okay let's get started!" did I snap back into focus, pencil and paper looming at me.

Confused, yet being a somewhat confident child, I simply asked my friend what we were doing. With her inner thoughts radiating 'Did you not just listen? The teacher just explained it to us', she continued with slight frustration to relay to me our teacher's instructions.

Picking up on her emotions more so than what she was describing, I absorbed next to nothing of her explanation. So, with fear of sitting there too long, looking like an idiot and hesitant to ask her again, I took advantage of my next resource: my teacher.

At this stage my teacher assumed I understood the task at hand and was more than happy to get me started. So she wrote down for me the first line of my poem.

'There once was a man'

She then asked me what I would like to call this man. I thought for a moment and replied with my father's name "Harry!" She smiled and said "Great!"

'There once was a man called Harry'

Being regretful that I had not listened in the beginning, I continued to pretend that I understood. Yet my fear of being exposed only buried me even further into my poetry nightmare.

Walking back to my table, feeling concerned, I looked around to see the class happily working on their poems. Missing my opportunity to tell the teacher the truth - that I didn't know what I was doing - there was no way out now. Somehow, I had to write the rest of this thing called a poem, but how? I didn't even know what one was!

Sitting back at my desk contemplating how to get this done, I waited a while, observing a few of my classmates receiving help from the teacher. I thought, 'It's okay, I can just ask her again, after all she is here to help'.

I walked back up to her desk, quietly said that I did not know what else to write. She smiled and took my paper, thought for a second and wrote . . . .

'He often loved to carry'

Assuming that this would suffice in helping me complete the task, she told me to go sit back down and try to finish the rest. I went back to my desk and sat down. My friend was working away and had almost completed her poem. She looked up at me, confused at why I had only written two lines.

Getting slightly frustrated at this point and feeling even more stupid, I sat there in stress and silence trying to work out how I could get out of this mess and finish this thing called a poem. Coming up with nothing else, I decided to ask my teacher once *again*, despite anticipating she would be just a little annoyed.

Giving her some time to help the other students, I waited until she was free and then approached her for the third time. She looked discouraged that I still had not written anything down. Yet, with kindness she took my paper, thought for a moment then wrote . . .

'He carried six boxes'

She asked me what I thought should be in the boxes, and suggested it had to rhyme with boxes. I did not know what rhyming was, so I just stood there desperately hoping to come up with at least *something!* After a short time of waiting and acknowledging my distress, she rescued me, suggesting 'Foxes'. "Foxes rhymes with boxes" she said and started to write . . . .

'Full of vicious foxes'

I smiled with huge relief that the moment was over. I was filled with excitement at the thought of the assignment nearing completion, and probably at the thought of boxes full of foxes!

My teacher turned to me and said, "Now Sarah, you have had lots of help, so you need to write the last bit, okay?" I walked over to my desk and sat down, yet again feeling dejected. I had no faith in my ability to complete this stupid assignment.

My friend next to me had finished her poem and was sitting there quietly. Perhaps she might be willing to help me again? So I asked her and surprisingly this time she was happy to help; she picked up my paper and started to read . . . .

There once was a man called Harry,

He often loved to carry.

He carried six boxes full of vicious foxes . . . .

To which she said . . . . "And then he was as happy as Larry"

I thought 'BRILLIANT!' So I ran over to my teacher and blurted out the last line "AND THEN HE WAS AS HAPPY AS LARRY!"

She *loved* it and burst out laughing! She was ecstatic that after all the help she had given me, I ended it with the most brilliant line of the day! I felt chuffed. I did it! I somehow finished the assignment, having no idea what I was actually doing, and in the end I won her heart by making her laugh!

On Fridays our teacher gave out awards to the kids in the class for the special things that they had achieved throughout the week. Right at the end of the weekly awards she called out "and the last and greatest award goes to Sarah Connor . . . for writing the cleverest poem in the class!"

I was shocked!! Being the actress I was, I accepted with gratitude and absorbed all the kudos; all the while knowing that I didn't really deserve it. Looking out the corner of my eye I glanced at my friend (who the award actually belonged to). She seemed confused and a little disappointed. Her glare said it all . . . 'I came up with that line, that award should have really gone to me.'

From that day believed I was no good at writing and no good at school. So, I carried on using my charm and sense of humour to get me by, which still to this day has not failed me.

Little did I know that later in life I would be a natural poet, and would one day have a book of my own.

And here it is.

I dedicate this book to my Asian friend in Grade One. I do not remember your name, but thank you for saving my arse. The award should have gone to you.

The Journey

So the journey begins,
Light the way of your path
And darken the temptation of your sins.
For we are born to live in light and sleep in dark,
Love freely, love in many ways, but don't deceive,
Or love will leave a dirty mark.
A foggy haze, it becomes a maze,
Disregarded love leaves a stain impossible to move,
Concentrated love is a thick dose of food,
Hard to swallow but easy to smooth
And your soul it does soothe,
Absorbing the heartbreak guaranteed left behind.
Yes, love . . .
Love will make you blind,
Not seeing, only feeling where you are going,
Only keeps the emotional momentum flowing,
You're never in control because love is in front, towing,
But you're smiling; you see your seed is slowly growing,
At its own pace pulling you along,
Love is of its own race, love is of its own song.

Listen To Your Soul

Life only goes as far as you travel,
Sharing the experiences is the key to your journey.

Every comment creates a new fork,
It's only your decisions, your feet that make you walk.

The destination is never as far as it seems,
It is the journey that will live in your dreams.

Follow your heart and listen to your soul,
Love everything that lives
And already paid will be the price of your toll.

Heart Thing

The window is slowly closing,
Painfully, hesitantly, I watch it extending.
My heart is slowly mending,
My thoughts still bending,
Because my feelings are strongly fending.
For life they fight but closure is pulling tight,
One day soon my heart will shine once again so bright.

Success

All were born to succeed,
Or at least try because we feel the need.
Each day we try to add to our success,
But progress only extends when we confess or undress our souls
Our true selves.
The inner being that gives our body stealth.
And finding its meaning of existence,
Will result in reason for believing in our soul's wealth.
We only produce a little more than we receive,
Running on empty will only make life a harder heave.
Maybe acceptance of our progression,
Will make happiness a much more enjoyable obsession?
Life really has no meaning but the meaning of ourselves,
If your ability to accept is in order then so is your health.
Just remember, if your mind and body tell you
"You haven't made it."
Be aware that your soul has already won the race,
Found it's foundation and has already laid it.

Light

Flesh are we,
It's only flesh we see.
Once flesh dies,
Our souls fly free.
Look in the eyes,
It is our souls you will see,
The light that shines within you and me.

War

War will make humanity extremely poor,
Leaving us the reputation to make judgment,
On nothing more.

Illusive Perception

In one mirror, my bum looks big
And in the other, my bum looks small,
But take away the mirror; I can barely see my bum at all.
So am I short or am I tall?

For without any mirror,
How do I know what I really look like at all?
And is that reflection really the shape of me?

For in one mirror, I look really quite happy,
And in the other mirror, I look really quite tall,
But in the next mirror, I have no shape really at all.

So is it the mirrors that hold the true reflection of me?
Or is it me only seeing what I'm choosing to see?

Arm's Length

Holding people at arm's length,
For fear of them seeing inside of you,
Not realising that that action in itself,
Only makes you extremely see-through.

Butterflies And Angels

My mum once said to me,
"My friend, if you lay with pigs, you start to smell like them."
But the same saying goes; I believe this to be true.
That if you lay with butterflies and angels,
You will start to fly like them too.

Blessed Be The Day

No hellos, put-down comments, ego battles engaged.
The war of the mind is so rampant,
The heart trying desperately to have its say.
It sits back just waiting to be expressed in its whole,
Waiting to be free, to be open and to fly with the soul.

But how can it fly when there is a war going on?
Dodging hurtful bullets and poison words,
Wounded, trying desperately to pull itself along.

The passion, inspiration, and light slowly fades,
Some hearts don't survive; they turn to stone in their graves.
Hearts wanting to be connected, to be loved and engaged,
Hearts wanting to be expressed, to be open and to be saved.

Hearts needing to be healed, admired and free,
These hearts trying to survive amongst the war in you and me.
There is a battle with love, with family, with friends,
A battle against strangers, against life, against ourselves
. . . it never ends.

Blessed be the day when our hearts can fly free,
Where they can express themselves so open and truthfully.
Without poison arrows and bitter minds,
Without jealous ammunition and insecure war crimes.

Blessed be the day when we stop playing games,
games of power and those power games.
The games of judgement, selfishness, pride and greed,
The games we think that . . . . 'If we win, then we will succeed.'

Blessed be the day when our hearts can fly free
And blessed be the day when I can truly be me.

Government

The governments are supposed to be working for the people,
But all the people want is for it to be peaceful.

Open Hearts

Lonely is the heart that feels,
Living amongst hearts that are made out of steel.

Adelaide Drought

As the tears fell out of my eyes,
I looked up into the clear black skies,
And the stars started to dance.
On the way home I glanced, at two tall dead trees,
Who died because they were so overwhelmingly thirsty.

Hurt People

The people that are hurt . . . hurt people.

Sarah Connor

Free Will

Bouts of happiness and sadness and platforms in-between,
Looking only to find that not everything can be seen.

For even in the eye a part of the retina is blind-
A spot where only mystery lies, placed there by the divine.

If we cannot see we will continue to walk blindly.
Bumping into walls you whisper "Follow your heart!"
Yet a heart is hard to follow,
When it has many times been blown apart.

"Look after your body for it is the temple of your truth".
Yet this vehicle from heavenly rain has heavy rust in its roof.

You say,
"There is a plan but the ultimate blessing is your free will."

Yet I say now,
"I am tired and wish very much that I had taken the blue pill."

Perception

Climbing to higher heights,
All there is to see is different points of view.

Your Face, Your Name

It wasn't love that made me blind because now I can see,
There is a large part of you that just doesn't suit me.

You play such amazing games,
To you, people are just puppets - just faces, just names.
The thing that made me blind was your manipulative spell,
You made it all look like heaven,
Even though we were dancing through hell.

But once the spell faded away, I slowly awoke to see,
That the part you put on display was so incredibly ugly.
Because that part was fake, that part was just a game,
That part included your face and that part included your name.
It was of no substance, it just wasn't real,
It was simply a placebo, I just thought it made me feel.

Because the game you play, you play so well,
You have mastered this game, this game called 'The Love Spell'.

Like a puppet master pulling on strings,
But one day you will realise that people are not things,
To be pulled, to be tugged, to be thrown away,
To be dumped at your disposal, for a new puppet you must play.

These puppets are people with real faces, real names,
These puppets have real hearts that don't like playing games.
These puppets are people, just like you.
Treat them with respect and give them what is true,
Otherwise one day, those puppets, they will start playing you!

We Are All One

It is not happiness until everyone is.

Ego

I tend to rebel against almost everything these days,
For in most places the ego does lay.
Even in the most creative of worlds,
People often think they are better because . . .

Friendship

Make the decision Left. Or make the decision Right.
"Which way do I turn?"
You ask me, as we journey through your life.

"My Friend, turn on your headlights, and find a pretty song.
When you feel your inner music,
the journey doesn't seem so long."

"I will be with you, whichever way you choose,
whatever song you sing, classical, wild rock or the blues."

"But please don't get angry with me,
when you crash into that big tall tree."
For I hope one day you will remember,
I was the friend sitting next to you, gently helping you see.

The Mind In Love

You do all the things that say 'you love thee',
Like buying lavish gifts and make love passionately.

Yet you do not know what your heart has to say,
For too much of your head tends to get in the way.

Creativity

Creativity is as fragile as a butterfly's wings.

Buried Cries

Tonight is the night, before the next day,
A day where I choose to walk away.
So tired am I, for I cannot sleep no more.
I choose to walk through that illusive door.
Dark are your eyes, for buried deep are your cries.
Your spirit under lock and key.
For in this moment I now see, that you and I will never be.

Life Stories

Every story told is art.
For it is taken from the great creation of 'Someone's Life.'
Life is art.
Life is our creation.

Invisible Heart Cords

I gave you a letter giving you my heart,
You said it was not valid because I picked it apart.

But this morning I woke from dreaming of you,
And to say you did not have my heart, simply was not true.

For a letter is only symbolic, with many words that just say.
Yet I have realised now, that it's invisible,
What the heart chooses to give away.

The Spirit Of Nature

The flowers are in joy . . . as they dance in the wind.

The Scene

Who are you when you take off all your clothes?
When you deconstruct the energy built
To support your masked pose?

Who are you underneath all that tattooed skin?
Underneath all those drugs, cigarettes, sex and gin?
As Shakespeare did say -
"The world is your stage and you choose your players."
Yet in this fine act, I can still see the real you,
Underneath all your costumed layers.

Just be yourself, that is all you need to be.
De-robe from your costumes and set your heart free.

Money

Money is simply energy and just like love,
It will flow to you . . . if you let it.

Our Core

Our strength, always from the inside.
It is when we are broken that we learn to cry.
Yet our heart's home remains the same,
And even in death, we can choose to play again.

Young & Old

Tonight I find myself in a place
Where the spirits are restless,
And pain is written on everyone's face.
These days it is only the young and the old that I enjoy to see,
For they are far closer to heaven, than the rest near me.

Creative Faith

I can now see clearly,
All creative magic is inside me,
And Faith, the enchanted key.

I say the words and send it far beyond,
and always, it is sent back to me,
more powerful and illuminated than previously,
More astounding than I had ever imagined it before.

I am so grateful that I need not worry anymore.

Time

There is no time . . . just moments.

Freedom In Stillness

Running, running, we are all running.
But do we ever get anywhere?
Certainly not the place where we are meant to be.
Because it is only when we stop running that we truly see,
Peace in stillness is what sets us free.

Labels

I'm too big to fit into your little labelled box,
So please save us both the energy and do not even begin to try.

Sarah Connor

The Dance Of
The Wounded Heart

I opened my heart again to you,
And the sound of that beat, triggered your usual dance move.
Your first step was . . .
Away.

The Systems Blanket

Was life meant to be lived this way?
Going against our natural flow every single day?
Doing things we don't like, just to get paid.

Whole lives wasted, so many dreams unfulfilled.
Through fear, our human potential has been crushed,
almost killed.

The blanket of depression lays heavily over us,
Each patch sewn together through years of mistrust.

A patch that signifies dreams unfulfilled
A patch that signifies hurts not yet healed
A patch that was sewn through the fear on TV
Patches sewn together through years of misdeed.

It is time for us to stop sleeping under this suffocating blanket.
In fact, it is time for us to stop sleeping at all.

Karma

How much more healing must I do?
How much more karma must I shed to flourish in this lifetime?

Ascension

As our old world comes to an end,
We must let go completely our all.
For when our structures shed and our old ways fall,
Our hearts lift us to where they truly desire to be.

A place where all life, all creation,
No longer bound, but completely free.

Saying No

Humanity would consume my every minute if I let it.

Dreaming

Although in my dreamtime,
We have made love both passionately and completely,
It has never quite quenched the thirst that is you.

Everything

Everything leads to everything.

Open Your Heart

When your heart is in play,
You grow more beautiful every day.
When your heart is in love,
You anchor the divine intelligence,
From Up Above.

Losing Oneself

It's hard to work out who you truly are.
For from afar, your colours seem to shine through.

Yet up close, your smell differs, your colours change,
They seem to fade the closer I get to you.

My heart asks
"But why do her colours dim?"

And my Soul replies
"Because my friend, for too long she has submerged herself and marinated solely in him."

Healing Waters

Here, and over the many years,
I have cried fears' tears.

Each time after feeling lighter, more free.
Each time shedding the old,
And bringing myself closer . . .
Back to the real me.

The Thick Of Illusion

What is this life, where it seems that the things you so deeply
desire never come to be true?
Is this but a cruel joke that the Heavens play from up above,
In their own fun, at the expense of you?

I understand that lessons need to be learned.
I understand that wounds need to surface in order to heal.
Yet I do not understand this place here,
That everyone believes to be 'Real'.

I remember a land deep in the memory of me,
Where what a heart desired was sent directly to be.
Where love was not confined by rules and regulations,
Nothing was separate; there were no dividing nations.

Dreamlike is the memory of this place in many ways,
Yet I deeply yearn for this state, right here, in my physical days.

Actions – Always Louder

Deafened by your actions,
Your words become void.

What use is your talk, when not backed by your walk?

Freedom In Flight

Pulled in by your heart, yet pushed back by your hand.
How do you know where you are going,
when you don't even know where you stand?

But what you do know, deep down,
Is what your inner eye can see,
That this little bird's big heart won't ever be caged,
And always, it will remain FREE.

Comfort Zones

The Weak and Afraid,
Complaining of their bed . . . the one they themselves made.

For all people do is talk, too scared to face up to their fears.

Perhaps it has been too easy to lay in bed, for all these years?

Gratitude

The dawn has arrived,
Open your heart and open your eyes.
I say Thank you! Thank You! Thank you!

The darkest part of the night was scary, its true,
But now all I can say is Thank you!

Jinpan Orange

Childlike in your play,
You stand aside as your eyes take flight.
Girl, let this world be your stage.

Like the small thin thread that hangs from your floral dress.
You are a brilliant tapestry woven from pure Goddess.

Garden Of Life

Seeds can be planted many a time,
Yet most of the time we neglect to let them grow.
Perhaps it's because we are sour with the taste of limes?
Not every seed is sour; it's the fruit we choose to pick.

Good seeds sprout every hour and the clock continues to tick.
Bad fruit makes you sick.
It's your choice, what you choose to pick.

For you are the gardener of your soul.

Self Love

Find your own beauty first, so another can enjoy it with you.

Third Person

Little man whose air is of knowing it all,
Yes you *may* be right, but you are not tall.
Your history has brought you much experience, this is true.
Yet there is still much imperfection,
Leaking out from inside of you.

You claim to be a good man, yet you crumple all the flow,
Believing you are right, but it is only what you know.
Perhaps if you weren't such a controlling arsehole
You would see,
That each soul needs to make their own unique choices,
So they can be.

I made a mistake; this is true.
I was bold, courageous and blind, and this affected you.
Yet, if you had laid down your sword and opened your eyes,
You would have seen my intention
And heard the pain of my cries.

It is not true what you said, that this burden is solely mine.
But I will stand here and take responsibility for this crime.

Although my actions were wrapped in a selfish film, this is true,
My intention was never meant to hurt the centre of you.

There was a whole play that you did not see,
For it wasn't played in front of you intentionally.
Perhaps you had felt this from time to time?
Yet believed that from our love,
It was impossible to commit such a crime?

No crime was committed; this you will never see.
However there were certainly feelings there,
On both sides, that were felt secretly.
These feelings built up like mildew over time,
Yet because they were secret,
They were hard to define.

A Ground-Crew Mission

So many tears cried in silence,
Yet I am crying once again.
I stand here before you O'Lord,
And the heart I will defend.

Yet although I feel the hand of change chipping but away,
Lord I cannot fight this no more,
I do not want to stay.

This energy is so old and so hard.
Where are those fighting for this side?

And now after so long,
I am left here with no more places to hide.

What is it you want me to do here Father?
When will this battle end?
There is only one thing I have learnt here Mother . . .
That this steel cold world is no longer my friend.

Crying in silence, I live on.

Insecurities

If you don't tame and defeat your insecurities,
They will tame and defeat you.

Connections Of The Heart

You entered my heart . . .
To this day you have never left.

Yet buried are my feelings for you,
For, to move on, I must forget.

Vulnerability

Most hearts that are closed have walls built of steel.

Yet with such walls,
It makes it virtually impossible for them to heal.

The Illusion

The mind in fear is weak,
Yet thinks itself so mighty and strong.

The mind in fear is cowardly, and believes it is never wrong.

The mind in fear is loud and tends to yell all the time.
The mind in fear speaks only of
Me me me, mine mine mine.

The mind in fear is hollow and it does not see,
How easily filled it is with unhealthy and vicious energy.

And because, at times, the mind in fear is blind,
It does not recognise anything outside its own kind.

Too consumed in itself and earthly erratic debris,
Little can it see, how easily and beautifully, it can be set free.

For the mind is just a tool for this Earth-Walk of ours,
A Veil Of Illusion - the one of disconnection and separated
hearts.

Change

The shift only comes in the doing
Of that which you are complaining about.
Stop complaining, start doing.

Loved In This Way Or That

Born into hell, I struggled to see,
A love that was meant to be for me.

So in my maimed desperation, I pulled on every intriguing face,
Hoping they could fill that void, my empty space.

Clawing them down till they ran away,
Realising now it was only my pain.

Pride

Pride can be beautiful when set upon an open and loving heart.
Yet when its foundation is one of stone,
It is as ugly as a gargoyle and always alone.

The Never-Ending Hoard

I dare you to put down your phones for one day,
To step outside, take a deep cleansing breath
and hear what this Earth has to say.

I dare you to interact from your heart,
To have the courage to speak your truth,
And if you don't agree, then don't take part.

I dare you to stand up against the crowd,
No matter who your friends.
Stand tall, be strong, and your truth defend.

I dare you to disconnect from this rat race, if only for a day.
To stop it all, and have the heart to see,
That we've all been led astray.

What is it anyway, that we are racing towards?
This competition, this game called 'The Never-Ending Hoard'.

Take, take, take, consume, consume, consume.
Do you not see we are running out of room?

We can't stop, because imbedded in our psyche,
Is "You ain't cool until you buy this brand of Nike"
Yet little do we realise that our wealth is inside.
All our power and our beauty we have been taught to hide.

All we need to do is stop and be still;
Listen . . . if only for one day . . .
Your soul, through its heart, has so much to say.
You make the choice for this Earth
When you purchase something you do not need.
We make the choice every day, the choice of faith or greed.

The richest man in the graveyard is what we are racing towards.
So I dare you to stop, to stop this Never-Ending Hoard.

Ugly Duckling

There lives a girl inside a woman whose beauty is of the swan.
With a heart so big and love so grand,
She could swallow her own pond.

As a child she played, innocent and free,
Accepting all that was beautiful and all that was ugly.

As she grew and watched all take flight,
flying off into the world.
Some were truly adorned in grace,
Some with an abundance of curls.

But this little girl did not feel she was the same,
For the other ducks in her pond, would call her ugly names.
Defeated and beaten and confused for the reasons why,
She held down this little girl as she grew,
And would not let her cry.

Little did she know, in time she would grow
To be the most beautiful of them all . . .

With a smile so wide and eyes so bright
Her wings expanded the world.
As she learnt to fly, she swooped in her arms,
That innocent little girl,
Holding her tight and in mid flight
Showed her the beauty of the world.

Faith

Faith equals freedom.

Fear Versus Love

When you judge me you have no room to love me.
You judge me because you do not understand,
You are afraid to step within yourself,
Afraid to trust and take my hand.

When I speak, you look at me confused, puzzled and afraid.
It seems I speak another language,
Yet deep down you understand what I say.

But your mind starts to shout
"Go behind enemy lines, this is a serious battle!"
So with fear your flag, you listen to the shouts
And wave your soldiers in like cattle.

Your friends, family and all that you can,
Stand to guard you with their one sided information.

They blindly charge and fight, extending all of their might
To the so-called 'enemy'.

If they stopped for one second, they would see,
That this so called enemy . . . loves you, so incredibly.

Old Friends

Time seems to be the healer, but in fact, it is actually his invisible old friend - Forgiveness.

Holding Another's Heart

Blindly walking into and destroying your House Of Cards . . .

Then foolishly, selfishly and clumsily trying to rebuild it with my honey soaked fingers.

Goodbye

I say goodbye to you now, in faith that we will meet again.
Perhaps not in this lifetime, but in another.
Will I know it is you? Will you remember me?

My heart calls out with sadness
Of all the mysteries I do not know, nor understand.
I feel alone and scared, for I am in this life but mere human.

One who hurts others, one who makes mistakes,
One who is lost, and one who's heart aches.

Please Lord, show me my way, my path
And help me forgive my mistakes.
For the pain of goodbye; my heart breaks.

I do not know if I will see you again, but I say goodbye now
And please know that I am truly sorry my friend.

The Essence Of Dreams

Pour your soul out into the garden of your dreams and watch them grow.

Marriage Of Control

A lost little girl with the most beautiful lips,
Bound to a man who lives in the Ego's abyss.

Where his words are all he knows,
And game is all he throws.
And you . . . his doll,
Trying to rest in the hands of his violent control.

Set Yourself Free

As we walk towards our dreams,
We release the hooks attached to our pain.

Pulling up the plugs, and letting all drain.
It is then after many tears, fighting your inner fears,
We become lighter and free.

It is then that we begin to fly and learn just to be.

Keep walking.

Uniquely Awesome

It is evident now from all that I have seen,
That I am that I am
And you be who you be.

Two Broken Hearts

You sit in your self-hatred every day and every night,
And from that self-hatred you project blame and fight.
And there, a small child sits and watches your every move,
Absorbing and learning from you, her own inner groove.

I love this small child, for I see myself in her,
A child who's emotional programming
was learnt from self-loathing slur.

And as you drive your wedge between her and I,
Two broken hearts begin to cry.

For in your self-hatred, you believe this to be true,
That no amount of poisoning has ever come from you.

Magically Free

I ride the Winds Of Faith from here to there
And without a care I set myself free, magically.

No One Is The Same

My shape is my shape, my hand, my hand.
My footprint that shapes uniquely the sand.
My voice, like no other, my dance the same.

I am the only ME that plays the way I play- this Earthly Game.
My name; not important. Nor is my face.
It is the soul that lights this vessel, in all her saving grace.

I AM THAT I AM & God . . . is me.
So now in this moment, I choose just to be.

Healing

You have to empty the sadness out of your heart first,
Before you can let the happiness in.

Sarah Connor

Breaking The Mould

How does man really know the journey of one's soul?
For all the ideas that fill the books, shaping us into mould.

And when the heart calls aloud, to gently guide us home,
It stirs the boundaries of this mould, shaking us to our bones.

And in those broken cracks can grow
Guilt and fears not yet known.
But its only when we break this mould,
Do we truly learn the flow.

It is then we plant our faith-filled seeds
And sit back to watch them grow,
Sprouting up divinity - bursting gardens of shine,
effervescence and glow.

The Brave

Deep, deep down at the very bottom of Pandora's Box
Lies a treasure; a jewel so great that it feeds wondrous growth
And wondrous change.

Yet to find this treasure one must firstly open the Box
And dive blindly into the depths of one's soul.

Not My Land

I came here drifting, from out-of-space,
Land. Where am I? What the hell is this place?
I don't recognise any of these lonely faces,
These broken hearts and these abstract spaces.
I have tried for many years,
walking vast scapes of dry desert land,
Only in the end to find tears.
In my heart - only sand.

I must now understand, that this scape in not my land.
So walk I must till I find the portal of peace,
Everyday surviving these insane streets.
Shutting my ears to the sound of screaming hearts,
Just like the war in the Middle East - darts
. . . . shoot from each other's minds,
Vicious insecure war crimes,
I can't stop till I find . . . .
Peace.

Queens And Kings

I am that I am and I be who I be,
And no one on this Earth can tell me how to be.
It is time to open our hearts and spread our wings,
For we are *all* Queens and we are *all* Kings.